Summa of

Strength in Stillness...
Bob Roth

GW00871047

Conversation Starters

By BookHabits

Bonus Downloads
Get Free Books with __Any Purchase__ of Conversation Starters!

Every purchase comes with a FREE download!

Add spice to any conversation
Never run out of things to say
Spend time with those you love

Get it Now

or Click Here.

Scan Your Phone

Tips for Using Conversation Starters:

EVERY GOOD BOOK CONTAINS A WORLD FAR DEEPER THAN the surface of its pages. Questions herein are designed to bring us beneath the surface of the page and invite us into the world that lives on. These questions can be used to:

- Foster a deeper understanding of the book
- Promote an atmosphere of discussion for groups
- Assist in the study of the book, either individually or corporately
- Explore unseen realms of the book as never seen before

Table of Contents

Introducing *Strength in Stillness*

*S*trength in Stillness is an elaboration of Transcendental Meditation, particularly its effects and benefits, as explained by its long time practitioner and teacher Bob Roth. Roth has taught Transcendental Meditation to celebrities, industry leaders, students and professionals after learning from Maharishi Mahesh Yogi in the 1970s. In this book, he shares his deep knowledge of the practice and his experience in teaching it to thousands of students who have learned and applied the method to improve their lives.

The book opens with Roth giving an account of how he got started with meditation in the 1960s. He describes himself as the person not most likely to be lured into sitting still and quietly going deep. He ignored a friend's suggestion that he take up meditation because he would rather be actively involved in changing the world, become a lawyer and then a senator who will implement social change. But as his life got busier and faster-paced, he turned to meditation to help deal with his mental and physical health challenges. He was surprised to find that meditation helped him manage his energy levels and mental alertness. He decided to train with Maharishi Mahesh Yogi for an extended time, taking a break from his studies. His training included learning from his teacher and scientists -- psychologists, medical doctors, neurologists-- who explained the mechanics and science of consciousness and how it affects the body. He saw how creativity and intelligence are related to pursuing social ideals. The technique of transcending or accessing the stillness within was taught.

Roth believes that there has been an increasing interest in meditation in recent years because of the epidemic of stress that affects too many people in modern society. This stress has resulted to physical and mental ailments including heart diseases, immune diseases, anxiety, and depression. A second reason for the increasing interest in meditation is that there is no known pill that can immediately cure stress. And the third reason is that science has increasingly proven that meditation can help manage stress. Meditation helps to achieve inner stillness, focus and clarity. Roth explains the benefits of TM and how this is to be practiced in order to fully experience its advantages.

The book is divided into three parts or what Roth calls the three pillars: the TM technique and how it works, the scientific explanations that show how and why TM works, and stories of how TM practitioners benefit from their meditation practice. The first part clarifies what TM is and what it is not. It is different from other forms of meditation and

Roth stresses the essence of the inner state of deep relaxation and alertness that one feels. He calls this transcending. Roth explains that the process and technique involves 20 minutes of meditation ideally before breakfast and another 20 minutes later in the day. A teacher gives a mantra which will be used with the meditation. He dispels notions of sitting in a special position, visualizations, or breath control and says these are not needed. His students come from different religions or practice no religion at all. The second part answers questions about the expected health benefits that practitioners have when they do the meditation. Research studies on medical and brain functions are featured to show how the body responds to meditation and how this leads to healing. The third part is written in collaboration with Roth's students, ranging from high profile CEOs to artists, students, and veterans. They share their experience in TM and how this has improved their lives. It serves to inspire and guide readers who are about to start TM or who want to take their practice further. Roth's own experience is shared as well. Roth writes in a conversational tone that is personal in approach. There is honesty in his words as he reveals important aspects of his life. There is much scientific data presented as he discusses the effects of TM. The reader will expect discussions about the brain and its functions, brain waves, physiology, psychology and related terms. Roth is specific about the scientific information he presents which result to a convincing argument about the effectiveness of TM. Stories, subtitled Meditative Moments, are personal accounts of Roth's students who tell how it feels to practice TM and how their day is improved by spending the morning and afternoon meditation sessions.

Strength in Stillness is a *New York Times* bestseller. Celebrities like Ellen DeGeneres, Hugh Jackman, and Cameron Diaz attest to the effective TM technique which has helped them deal with their life struggles and crises.

Discussion Questions

"Get Ready to Enter a New World"

Tip: Begin with questions dealing with broader issues to ensure ample time for quality discussions. Read through all discussion questions before engaging.

~~~

question 1

The book opens with Roth giving an account of how he got started with meditation in the 1960s. What was his initial reaction to encountering Transcendental Meditation?

~~~

~~~

question 2

He studied TM from Maharishi Mahesh Yogi. What convinced him that TM is effective?

~~~

~~~

question 3

Scientists were among his teachers, along with Maharishi Mahesh Yogi. What part did they do in his training?

~~~

~~~

question 4

There has been an increasing interest in meditation in recent years. Why is this so?

~~~

question 5

The book is divided into three parts or what Roth calls the three pillars. What are these three?

~~~

question 6

Roth explains the difference of TM from other forms of meditation. What is the difference?

~~~

~~~

question 7

The technique involves 20 minutes of meditation before breakfast and another 20 minutes later in the day. Why is 20 minutes specified?

~~~

~~~

question 8

There are health benefits that practitioners experience when they do the meditation. What are these health benefits?

~~~

~~~

question 9

CEOs, artists, students, and veterans share their experience in TM and how this has improved their lives. Whose stories do you particularly like? Why?

~~~

~~~

question 10

Roth writes in a conversational tone. What effect does this have on readers? Do you like his tone?

~~~

~~~

question 11

Discussions about the brain and its functions, brain waves, physiology, psychology and related terms are included. Why does Roth include lots of scientific information?

~~~

~~~

question 12

Meditative Moments are personal accounts of Roth's students who tell how it feels to practice TM. Whose accounts do you like? Do their stories change your initial attitudes towards TM? In what way?

~~~

~~~

question 13

Roth's students come from different religions or practice no religion at all. Why does religion make no difference in studying TM?

~~~

~~~

question 14

Science has increasingly proven that meditation can help manage stress. How does it help people deal with stress?

~~~

~~~

question 15

A teacher gives a mantra which will be used with the meditation. How will a mantra help in meditation?

~~~

~~~

question 16

Billionaire investment banker Ray Dalio says TM is the reason behind all of his successes. How does TM help one become successful?

~~~

~~~

question 17

Actor Hugh Jackman says TM helped his son through a difficult time. Would you recommend TM to young people? Why? Why not?

~~~

~~~

question 18

Publishers Weekly says Roth's book is "well-argued." Why does it say this? How does Roth support his claims about TM?

~~~

~~~

question 19

A Goodreads review thinks that the book is devoid of the actual instructions on how to meditate and that it is just a marketing ploy to get people to enroll in a TM course. Do you agree? What about the book that makes you want to enroll in TM?

~~~

~~~

question 20

An Amazon review likes the book because it is personal and has stories about real people. How do the stories affect you? Are you convinced of TM's effect because of the stories?

~~~

Introducing the Author

Bob Roth is the CEO of David Lynch Foundation, a nonprofit organization that teaches Transcendental Meditation to help people manage stress in their lives. The foundation has reached hundreds of thousands of children worldwide belonging to underserved populations, war veterans who suffer post-traumatic stress, and survivors of domestic violence. Roth has been teaching TM for 45 years, and has clients from all walks of life including Fortune 100 CEOs, and celebrities like Oprah Winfrey, Michael J. Fox, and Ellen DeGeneres.

Roth always thought that he would enter politics one day. His family is highly political and he was brought up with the notion that he will help change the world for the better. He went to University of California, Berkely where he got involved in student protests that increasingly became violent. He was actively involved in the presidential campaign of Robert F. Kennedy as a senior in high school. The deaths of Martin Luther King, Jr. And Robert F. Kennedy in 1968 gave him the urgency to become a politician. But his goal to become a Senator slowly changed as he got disappointed with the divisive politics of his times. He soon changed his plans to become an educator instead. He thought he would be able to make significant changes in society by molding young minds. While in college, Roth was often troubled by thoughts of not being happy enough. He observed that successful people were too stressed to enjoy the fruits of their labor. As a student he had high stress levels, had memory lapses, and had disturbed sleep patterns. He noticed a man named Peter Stevens who was smart, calm, centered and energetic and learned that he practiced meditation. He got curious. Things became too difficult and he finally decided to try TM after initially rejecting the idea. He found the results very helpful and few years afterwards, he took a six-month leave from his college studies to train in teaching TM with Maharishi Mahesh Yogi in Spain. Thus started his lifelong devotion to teach

TM to others who needed it. Today, he is a much sought speaker for big events like Aspen Ideas Festival, Google Zeitgeist, Summit, and Wisdom2.0. Having taught so many industry leaders, he opened the Center for Leadership Performance to further provide them training.

Roth is concerned that the stress epidemic is not only affecting adults but children as well. He recounts how surprised he was when a classroom of second-grade students all admitted to experiencing stress after Roth described what stress is. He says nowadays stress is not limited to children suffering poverty and violence. Society is pressuring kids to catch up with adult demands and this has resulted to doctors reporting an increase in stress-related ailments among kids from affluent homes. People who approach him for meditation lessons are all ready to try a new approach to manage stress because they have tried medical prescriptions and they have not been effective in the long term. This is the reason why, Roth says, TM continues to interest people.

Bonus Downloads
*Get Free Books with **Any Purchase** of* Conversation Starters!

Every purchase comes with a FREE download!

Add spice to any conversation
Never run out of things to say
Spend time with those you love

Get it Now

<u>or Click Here.</u>

Scan Your Phone

Fireside Questions

"What would you do?"

Tip: These questions can be a fun exercise as it spurs creativity among the readers by allowing alternate scene endings and "if this was you" questions.

question 21

Bob Roth is the CEO of David Lynch Foundation, a nonprofit organization that teaches Transcendental Meditation to help people manage stress in their lives. Who are the people that benefit from this foundation?

~~~

~~~

question 22

Roth always thought that he would enter politics one day. Why did he change his mind about becoming a politician?

~~~

~~~

question 23

He took a six-month leave from his college studies to train in teaching TM with Maharishi Mahesh Yogi in Spain. What made him decide to pursue TM? Do you think he made the right decision?

~~~

~~~

question 24

Roth is concerned that the stress epidemic is not only affecting adults but children as well. What causes stress among children today?

~~~

~~~

question 25

People who approach him for meditation lessons are all willing to try a new approach to stress management. Why? What is the usual approach to healing stress that has often failed?

~~~

~~~

question 26

Roth wanted to become a Senator but decided to pursue teaching meditation instead. If he followed his original plan to become a politician, what kind of person would he be today?

~~~

~~~

question 27

Roth writes in a conversational tone. If he used a formal voice how would it change the book?

~~~

~~~

question 28

He includes stories of his students who share experiences of how meditation is changing their lives. If the stories were not included, how interesting would the book be? Would you still read it?

~~~

~~~

question 29

Scientific research on TM are cited in the book. If Roth lessened the use of scientific language would it still be credible? How important is the use of scientific information?

~~~

~~~

question 30

Hollywood celebrities attest to Roth's excellent teaching. If the book did not cite the experiences of celebrities, how would it affect the book's popularity? Would you still want to read it?

~~~

Quiz Questions

"Ready to Announce the Winners?"

Tip: Create a leaderboard and track scores to see who gets the most correct answers. Winners required. Prizes optional.

~~~

quiz question 1

Roth studied TM under the guidance of his teacher
_____.

~~~

~~~

quiz question 2

TM involves the technique of transcending or accessing the _____ within.

~~~

~~~

quiz question 3

Roth says the epidemic of _____ has resulted to physical and mental ailments including heart diseases, immune diseases, anxiety, and depression.

~~~

~~~

quiz question 4

True or False: There is no pill that can cure stress.

~~~

~~~

quiz question 5

True or False: Meditation helps to achieve inner stillness, focus and clarity.

~~~

~~~

quiz question 6

True or False: TM involves 30 minutes of meditation ideally before breakfast and another 30 minutes later in the day.

~~~

~~~

quiz question 7

True or False: The book's Meditative Moments feature personal accounts of Roth's students who tell how it feels to practice TM.

~~~

~~~

quiz question 8

Bob Roth is the CEO of _____, a nonprofit organization that teaches Transcendental Meditation to help people manage stress in their lives.

~~~

~ ~ ~

quiz question 9

When he was young, he was actively involved in the presidential campaign of _____.

~ ~ ~

~ ~ ~

quiz question 10

True or False: While in college, he noticed a man named Peter Stevens who was smart, calm, centered and energetic and learned that he practiced meditation.

~ ~ ~

~~~

quiz question 11

True or False: Roth is concerned that the stress epidemic is not only affecting adults but children as well.

~~~

~~~

quiz question 12

True or False: Roth is CEO of the foundation that teaches meditation to underserved children, war veterans who suffer post-traumatic stress, and survivors of domestic violence.

~~~

Quiz Answers

1. Maharishi Mahesh Yogi
2. stillness
3. stress
4. True
5. True
6. False
7. True
8. David Lynch Foundation
9. Robert F. Kennedy
10. True
11. True
12. True

Ways to Continue Your Reading

EVERY month, our team runs through a wide selection of books to pick the best titles for readers and reading groups, and promotes these titles to our thousands of readers – sometimes with free downloads, sale dates, and additional brochures.

Click here to sign up for these benefits.

If you have not yet read the original work or would like to read it again, you can purchase the original book here.

Bonus Downloads
*Get Free Books with **Any Purchase** of* Conversation Starters!

Every purchase comes with a FREE download!

Add spice to any conversation
Never run out of things to say
Spend time with those you love

Get it Now

or Click Here.

Scan Your Phone

On the Next Page...

If you found this book helpful to your discussions and rate it a 4 or 5, please write us a review on the next page.

Any length would be fine but we'd appreciate hearing you more! We'd be very encouraged.

Till next time,

BookHabits

"Loving Books is Actually a Habit"

Lightning Source UK Ltd.
Milton Keynes UK
UKHW011307150720
366585UK00002B/385